MORNING HAIKU

Morning
Haiku

Sonia Sanchez

Beacon Press, Boston

Beacon Press
25 Beacon Street
Boston, Massachusetts 02108-2892
www.beacon.org

Beacon Press books
are published under the auspices of
the Unitarian Universalist Association of Congregations.

The following were previously published: "14 haiku (for
Emmett Louis Till)," *Southern Quarterly* 45, no. 4 (Summer 2008);
"21 haiku (for Odetta)," *Harvard Review* 36 (Spring 2009); "1 year
after 9/11," *Philadelphia Sunday Inquirer Magazine*, September 8,
2002; "10 haiku (for Philadelphia Murals)," in *More Philadelphia
Murals and the Stories They Tell*, Jane Golden, Robin Rice, Natalie
Pompilio (Philadelphia: Temple University Press, 2006).

13 12 11 10 8 7 6 5 4 3 2 1

This book is printed on acid-free paper that meets the uncoated
paper ANSI/NISO specifications for permanence as revised in
1992.

Text design and composition by M. F. Rutherglen
at Wilsted & Taylor Publishing Services

Library of Congress Cataloging-in-Publication Data
Sanchez, Sonia.
  Morning haiku / Sonia Sanchez.
    p. cm.
  ISBN 978-0-8070-6910-3 (hardcover : alk. paper)
  1. Haiku, American. 2. African Americans—Poetry. I. Title.
  PS3569.A468M67 2010
  811'.54—dc22   2009027670

Let me wear the day
Well so when it reaches you
You will enjoy it.

Sonia Sanchez

The best thing you can do is to be a woman and stand before the world and speak your heart.

Abbey Lincoln

contents

haikuography

From the moment i found a flowered book high up
on a shelf at the 8th Street Bookshop in New York
City, a book that *announced* Japanese haiku; from the
moment i opened that book, and read the first haiku,
i slid down onto the floor and cried and was changed.
i had found *me*. It's something to find yourself in a
poem—to discover the beauty that i knew resided
somewhere in my twenty-one-year-old bloodstream;
from the moment i asked the clerk in the bookstore
if i was pronouncing this haiku word correctly, i knew
that i had discovered me, had found an awakening,
an awareness that i was connected not only to nature,
but to the nature of myself and others; from the mo-
ment i saw the blood veins behind beautiful eyes,
the fluids in teeth, and the enamel in tongues, i knew
that haiku were no short-term memory, but a long
memory.

Patricia Donegan shares the idea of "haiku mind"—
"a simple yet profound way of seeing our everyday
world and living our lives with the awareness of the
moment expressed in haiku—and to therefore hope-

fully inspire others to live with more clarity, compassion, and peace."

i knew when i heard young poets say in verse and conversation: i'm gonna put you on "pause," i heard their "haiku nature," their haikuography. They were saying, i gotta make you slow down and check out what's happening in your life. In the world.

So this haiku slows us down, makes us stay alive and breathe with that one breath that it takes to recite a haiku.

This haiku, this tough form disguised in beauty and insight, is like the blues, for they both offer no solutions, only a pronouncement, a formal declaration—an acceptance of pain, humor, beauty and non-beauty, death and rebirth, surprise and life. Always life. Both always help us to maintain memory and dignity.

What i found in the 8th Street Bookshop was extraordinary and *ordinary*: Silence. Crystals. Cornbread and greens. Laughter. Brocades. The sea. Beethoven. Coltrane. Spring and winter. Blue rivers. Dreadlocks. Blues. A waterfall. Empty mountains. Bamboo. Bodegas. Ancient generals. Lamps. Fireflies. Sarah Vaughan—her voice exploding in the universe, returning to earth in prayer. Plum blossoms. Silk and steel. *Cante jondo.* Wine. Hills. Flesh. Perfume. A breath inhaled and held. Silence.

And i found that my mouth and the river are one and the same.

> i set sail
> in tall grass
> no air stirs.

Sonia Sanchez

MORNING HAIKU

10 haiku

(for Max Roach)

1.

Nothing ends
every blade of grass
remembering your sound

2.

your sounds exploding
in the universe return
to earth in prayer

3.

as you drummed
your hands kept
reaching for God

4.

the morning sky
so lovely imitates
your laughter

5.

you came warrior
clear your music
kissing our spines

6.

feet tapping
singing, impeach
our blood

7.

you came drumming
sweet life on
sails of flesh

8.

your fast beat
riding the air settles
in our bones

9.

your drums
soloing our breaths into
the beat...unbeat

10.

your hands
shimmering on the
legs of rain.

duende

1.

My hands
abandon me
to bloodletting

2.

my breasts
are dancing in
silver

3.

my feet
are crying
blues

4.

my thighs
sing the flesh
off the guitar

5.

my breath
is indecent as
my teeth

6.

aaaaaahhhhhhh
yeyeyeyeyeye
i am still standing...

dance haiku

1.

Do we dance
death in a fast lane
of salsa

2.

or minuet
death with an aristocrat's
pointed toe

3.

do we ease
into death with
workingclass abandon

4.

or position our
legs in middleclass
laughter

5.

do we swallow
death in a fast gulp
of morning pills

6.

or factor death
into prime years
in our throats?

14 haiku

(for Emmett Louis Till)

1.

Your limbs buried
in northern muscle carry
their own heartbeat

2.

Mississippi...
alert with
conjugated pain

3.

young Chicago
stutterer whistling
more than flesh

4.

your pores
wild stars embracing
southern eyes

5.

footprints blooming
in the night remember
your blood

6.

in this southern
classroom summer settles
into winter

7.

i hear your
pulse swallowing
neglected light

8.

your limbs
fly off the ground
little birds...

9.

we taste the
blood ritual of
southern hands

10.

blue midnite
breaths sailing on
smiling tongues

11.

say no words
time is collapsing
in the woods

12.

a mother's eyes
remembering a cradle
pray out loud

13.

walking in Mississippi
i hold the stars
between my teeth

14.

your death
a blues, i could not
drink away.

10 haiku

(for Philadelphia Murals)

1.

Philadelphia roots
lighting these walls
with fireflies

2.

flowers stretched
in prayer on a
cornerstone wall

3.

brownskinned
children dancing
with butterflies

4.

these children's
faces humiliate
the stars

5.

Philadelphia
painted with
blue hallelujahs

6.

winter
a warrior's face
i hear our bones singing

7.

in the open
alley a galaxy
of dreams

8.

common ground
is we, forever
breathing this earth

9.

hands
in the green light
saluting peace

10.

even in the
rain, these murals
pause with rainbows.

4 haiku

(for Nubia)

1.

Telephone wires sang
her voice over
soft sister laughter

2.

you held us
with summer stained
smiles of hope

3.

i hold your
breath today...you sail home
across the ocean

4.

i see you Nubia
walking your Mississippi walk
God in your hands.

21 haiku

(for Odetta)

1.

The sound of
your voice thundering out
of the earth

2.

a drum
beat summoning us
to prayer

3.

behold
the smell of
your breathing

4.

dilated
by politics
you dared to love

5.

you opened
up your throat
to travellers

6.

exhaled
Lead Belly on Saturday
nites and Sunday mornings

7.

your music asked:
has your song a father
or a mother?

8.

on stage
you were a
soldier of hands

9.

accenting
beat after beat
into beauty

10.

you asked: is there
no song that will
bring rain to this desert?

11.

you unveiled
your voice at early
demonstrations

12.

saluted our
blood until we were
no longer strangers

13.

waltzed our
eyes until we danced
from chandeliers

14.

your songs journeyed
in a country padlocked
with greed

15.

a country
still playing on
adolescent knees

16.

suddenly the morning
takes you back   another
time another continent

17.

where stones
contacted stars   told
us hello and goodbye

18.

finally we remember
how you gave life
to memory

19.

remember your eyes
morning stars
perfumed with rain

20.

your mouth
a sweet wind
painted with hieroglyphics

21.

finally to pass
your song into our
ancestral rivers.

3 haiku

1.

(for Richard Long)

Elegant ascot
man turning words
into gems.

2.

(for Tanabata festival)

star filled poem
shall I hang you
on pine trees?

3.

(for Luisa Moreno)

Free brown woman
sailing white river currents
without a *mortgaged soul*.

4 haiku

(for Eugene Redmond)

1.

Blue atom
poet transcribing
our flesh

2.

your quicksilver
words waterfalling in
sweet confession

3.

you have taken down
the morning turned it into
a roar of blackness

4.

your poems...
butterflies fluttering down
to earth.

7 haiku

(for Ray Brown)

1.

African bass
translating our
beauty

2.

hammering
nails into the
off...beat...

3.

walking
our eyes on
water

4.

hands
violining us into
blue black waves

5.

ding ding ding (click)
dong dong dong dong dong (click)
dee boom (click) deeeboooom (click)
deeeee booooom (click)

6.

bass
transcending
old memory

7.

your sound
sweet perfume
on my thighs.

6 haiku

(for Beauford Delaney)

1.

("L'oiseau Charlie Parker")

I

An avalanche
of reds and pinks exploding
into jazz

II

this yardbird
wears ostrich feathers
no boundaries.

2.

(Untitled Watercolor)

Ragman
in Paris wearing
Harlem eyes.

3.

(Untitled)

How to dance
in blood and
remain sane?

4.

("Lithograph Afrique")

Pink and green and
grey figures leap off the ship
bones line the clouds.

5.

("Portrait of Ella Fitzgerald")

Nose. mouth. eyes.
green. orange.
yellow voice spinning...

6.

("Self-portrait")

    I

One eye larger
than the other swimming
in the Seine

    II

green-brown face
African neck brace, European
collar on pink body.

2 haiku

(on viewing John Dowell's Tranescape*)*

1.

Multicolored ribbons
blowing away space as
Trane paints his tune.

2.

man
in the stillness
of blue chords...

4 haiku

(for Max Roach)

1.

i need to
catch your brain
and steady it

2.

let's impeach
this yellow detour
of your memory

3.

how dare
your sweet hands
forget you!

4.

i kiss the
surprise always in
your eyes.

sister haiku

(for Pat)

1.

How many
secrets you carried
in your panties

2.

infections
of confections
no retractions

3.

the autumnal
rain announced a
sister's fragrance

4.

your slanted
black eyes smiled
crystals

5.

can two little
girls holding hands walk unnoticed
in a large house?

6.

young man...home from war...
envies the subtle
pause of young beauty

7.

disguised as
uncle he picked at
your unbroken spine

8.

how to moisten
the silence of an
afternoon molestation?

9.

silk on your
skin no armor for
the amputee

10.

Birmingham
eyes ignoring
the winter's confinement

11.

to be born
to be raped
each journey a sudden wave

12.

his touch wore
you down to a
fugitive eye.

13.

the sound of you
sucking your thumb at nite
blows in my ears

14.

all morning
our mother's voice
beyond the hills.

15 haiku

(for Toni Morrison)

1.

We know so little
about migrations of souls crossing
oceans. seas of longing;

2.

we have not always been
prepared for landings that held
us suspended above our bones;

3.

in the beginning
there wuz we and they and others
too mournful to be named;

4.

or brought before elders
even held in contempt. they were
so young in their slaughterings;

5.

in the beginning
when memory was sound. there was
bonesmell. bloodtear. whisperscream;

6.

and we arrived
carrying flesh and disguise
expecting nothing;

7.

always searching
for gusts of life
and sermons;

8.

in the absence
of authentic Gods
new memory;

9.

in our escape from plunder
in our nesting on agitated land
new memory;

10.

in our fatigue at living
we saw mountains cracking
skulls, purple stars, colourless nights;

11.

trees praising our innocence
new territories dressing our
limbs in starched bones;

12.

in our traveling to weselves
in the building, in the journeying
to discover our own deaths;

13.

in the beginning
there was a conspiracy of blue eyes
to iron eyes;

14.

new memory falling into death
O will we ever know
what is no more with us;

15.

O will weselves ever
convalesce as we ascend into wave after
wave of bloodmilk?

5 haiku

(for Brother Damu)

1.

You pointed out
lewd waters mad
with toxic wounds

2.

you world traveller
mixing language
and touch

3.

we see your hands
bandaging disciples
of peace

4.

humming this
earth back
to sanity

5.

silk toned
dapper black
man smiling...

6 haiku

*(for Elizabeth Catlett
in Cuernavaca)*

1.

La Señora
making us remember
flesh and wind

2.

O how you
help us catch
each other's breath

3.

a woman's
arms climbing with
colored dreams

4.

Elizabeth
slides into the pool
hands kissing the water

5.

i pick
up your breath and
remember me

6.

your hands
humming hurricanes
of beauty.

5 haiku

1.

You sniff
dog-like around
language

2.

i taste
your saliva spiked
with applause

3.

painted beads
falling from your
fingertips

4.

poems
going the wrong way
in moonlight

5.

you fast talking
manicured poet
sailing on glass.

2 haiku

(for Ras Baraka)

1.

Your hands
shout eucalyptus
songs

2.

your poems
the smell of
morning rain.

6 haiku

(for Oprah Winfrey)

1.

O how we
rinse each other's
shadows

2.

summertime
roses caught in
our throats

3.

you
position women against
grave diggers

4.

in your laughter
we capture birthdays
in wild colors

5.

you have
rescued women from a
timid ground of loss

6.

in your eyes
we breathe each other's
dreams.

5 haiku

(for Sarah Vaughan)

1.

Me in midair
sailing underneath
your lips.

2.

we don't stare
we don't seem to care
are we a pair?

3.

where are the clowns
are they all stampeding
my house?

4.

without your
residential breath
i lose my timing.

5.

Send in the clowns
There is space
above the air.

2 haiku

1.

Your eyes
ignite...stampede
death

2.

your body turns
towards me
more than baptism.

9 haiku

(for Freedom's Sisters)

1.

(Kathleen Cleaver)

quicksilver
panther woman speaking
in thunder

2.

(Charlayne Hunter-Gault)

summer silk woman
brushing the cobwebs
off Southern legs

3.

(Shirley Chisholm)

We saw your
woman sound   footprinting
congressional hallways

4.

(Betty Shabazz)

your quiet face
arrived at a road
unafraid of ashes...

5.

(Fannie Lou Hamer)

feet deep
in cotton you shifted
the country's eyes

6.

(Barbara Jordan)

Texas star
carrying delicate words
around your waist

7.

(Rosa Parks)

baptizer of
morning light walking us away
from reserved spaces

8.

(Myrlie Evers-Williams)

you rescued women and men
from southern subscriptions
of death

9.

(Dr. Dorothy Irene Height)

I

your words
helped us reconnoiter
the wonder of women

II

woman sequestered
in the hurricane
of herstory...

5 love haiku

1.

Under
a sexual sky you
coughed swords

2.

your smell
slides under my
fingernails

3.

love
walking backwards
towards assassinations

4.

locust man
eating the grain
of women

5.

your tongue
jelly on my
lips.

7 haiku

(for St. Augustine)

1.

Playboy of North
Africa, burning the streets before
you learned to genuflect

2.

mama's boy
holding on to Saint
Monica's tits

3.

Milan
lover of sculpted
waists

4.

can i reinvent
your pigeon-toed walk
toward God?

5.

can i resurrect
sepulchers, posturing
inside your veins?

6.

can i
spill salt from
your legs?

7.

can i reinvent you and me
to love until i become still
to worship until you become stone?

6 haiku

(for Maya Angelou)

1.

You have
taught us how
to pray

2.

your poems
yellow tattoos on the
morning dew

3.

we dance
in the eye
of your pores

4.

in a sudden
pause of breath
secrets unlock

5.

you show us
how to arrange our
worldly selves

6.

your poems
a landscape of
seabirds.

haiku woman

(La mujer de los ojos)

1.

You...woman
surrendering your arms
to silk

2.

coming among
us luxurious with
flesh

3.

you allow no
frailty to accent
your blood

4.

you ... swallowing
the morning as you lean
back on your eyes.

memory haiku

1.

i was born
a three-legged
black child.

2.

carrying an
extra leg for quick
departures.

3.

beneath the sun
i moved in short
Birmingham breaths.

4.

silence of the
house...in the kitchen
someone washes the floor.

5.

silence. no words.
just the sound
of earthquakes.

6.

precocious morning
releasing an avalanche
of blood.

7.

in the hospital
mother, you chanted complex
half-moons.

8.

what is it about
childbirth that women
ask for seconds?

9.

how long the nite
to break your body into
a diabetic coma.

10.

how wild the
gust of blood running
down hospital corridors.

11.

do women
make a living singing
death prints?

12.

in my dreams
i rubbed your limbs
until they sparkled.

13.

wherever i am
i patrol
your seasonal death.

14.

i bring you
pine trees and laughter
for your journey.

15.

do you hear me
singing in the mountains
under a constant sky?

16.

i, a passerby
to your death,
cradle your breath.

17.

i, a sleepwalker
to dreams, imagine you a
crane flying south.

18.

every day
i hear your voice
beyond the hills.

haiku poem: 1 year after 9/11

Sweet September morning
how did you change skirts so fast?

What is the population of death
at 8:45 on a Tuesday morning?

How does a country become
an orphan to its own blood?

Will these public deaths
result in private bloodletting?

Amongst the Muslim, the Jew, and the Christian
whom does God love more?

How did you disappear, peace, without
my shawl to accompany you?

What *cante jondo* comes
from a hijacked plane?

Did you hear the galvanized steel
thundering like hunted buffalo?

Glass towers collapsing in prayer
are you a permanent guest of God?

Why do some days wear the
clothing of a beggar?

Where did these pornographic flames
come from, blaspheming sealed births?

Did they search for pieces of life
by fingerprinting the ash?

Death speaking in a loud voice,
are your words only for the deaf?

What is the language for bones
scratching the air?

What is the accent of life
when windows reflect only death?

Hey death! You furious frequent flier,
can you hear us tasting this earth?

Did the currents recognize her sound
as she sailed into the clouds?

Does death fly south
at the end of the day?

Did you see the burnt bones
sleepwalking a city?

Is that Moses. Muhammad. Buddha. Jesus.
gathering up the morning dead?

Why did you catch them, death,
holding their wings out to dry?

How did this man become
a free-falling soliloquy?

Why did September come whistling
through the air in a red coat?

How hard must the wind
blow to open our hearts?

How to reconnoiter our lives
away from epileptic dreams?

How to live—How to live
without contraband blood?

Is this only an eastern wind
registering signatures of ash?

Do the stars genuflect
with pity toward everyone?

explanatory notes

1   *Max Roach*, a founder of modern jazz, was a world-renowned African American percussionist, drummer, and composer.

9   *Emmett Louis Till* was a fourteen-year-old African American Chicagoan murdered in 1955 in Money, Mississippi, for allegedly flirting with a white woman.

15   *The Philadelphia Murals* are a public art project created by local artists and communities that reflect the culture of Philadelphia's neighborhoods. There are over a hundred murals throughout the city, including one of Sonia Sanchez.

19   *Nubia* was a dear friend of the poet who died quite unexpectedly. This poem was written for her funeral.

21   *Odetta* was a famed African American folk singer whose songs became anthems for the U.S. civil rights movement.

29   *Richard Long* is a celebrated African American scholar of literature, culture, and the arts. This poem was written on the occasion of a ceremony in his honor.

29 *"Tanabata"* is a poem written about stars and hung on trees.

30 *Luisa Moreno* was the first woman and first Latina member of the California Congress of Industrial Organizations Council and a leader in the United States labor movement.

31 *Eugene Redmond* is an African American poet from St. Louis.

33 *Ray Brown* was an African American jazz double bassist, considered by many to be a leading bassist in the bop style. This poem was written after listening to his music on the radio after his death.

37 *Beauford Delaney* was a renowned African American modernist painter. These haiku were written after viewing his work at the Philadelphia Museum of Art.

41 *John Dowell* is an African American artist. *Tranescape* is his painting of the famous jazz musician John Coltrane.

43 *"4 haiku (for Max Roach)"* were written after a visit to a residential home in Brooklyn.

51 *Toni Morrison* is a Nobel Prize–winning African American author. These haiku were written after reading Morrison's novel *Paradise*.

57 *Brother Damu* was one of the first African American environmental activists and peace workers. He was the founder of Black Voices for Peace and the National Black Environmental Justice Network.

59 *Elizabeth Catlett* is a major African American sculptor and printmaker in America and Mexico whose career spans the twentieth and twenty-first centuries. She lives in Cuernevaca, Mexico, and New York City.

63 A young African American poet, *Ras Baraka* is the son of poets Amiri and Amina Baraka.

65 *Oprah Winfrey* is an African American television host, a producer, and a philanthropist.

67 *Sarah Vaughan* was an African American jazz singer. These haiku were written while listening to a recording of Vaughan singing "Send in the Clowns."

71 *Freedom's Sisters* is a multimedia, interactive exhibition that brings to life twenty African American women who fought for the equality of people of color.

71 *Kathleen Cleaver* was active in the Black Panther Party and is a senior lecturer in law at Emory University.

71 *Charlayne Hunter-Gault* was the first African American student to integrate the University of Georgia. She is a prominent journalist.

72 *Shirley Chisholm* was the first African American woman elected to Congress, the first major-party African American candidate for president of the United States, and the first woman to run for the Democratic presidential nomination.

72 *Betty Shabazz* was a civil rights activist, a professor, and the wife of Malcolm X.

73 *Fannie Lou Hamer* was the vice-chair of the Mississippi

Freedom Democratic Party, a voting-rights activist, and a civil rights leader.

73 *Barbara Jordan* was an African American congresswoman from 1973 to 1979.

74 *Rosa Parks* was an African American civil rights activist whom the U.S. Congress called the "Mother of the Modern-Day Civil Rights Movement."

74 *Myrlie Evers-Williams* was the first full-time chairperson of the NAACP and is the widow of murdered civil rights leader Medgar Evers.

75 *Dr. Dorothy Irene Height* was president of the National Council of Negro Women from 1957 to 1997 and is a recipient of the Congressional Gold Medal.

79 *St. Augustine* was a philosopher and theologian born in North Africa of Berber descent who wrote *The Confessions*, often considered the first Western autobiography. These haiku were written after having spent a week sleeping in St. Augustine's room at a monastery.

83 *Maya Angelou* is an award-winning African American poet, memoirist, and best-selling author.

85 *La mujer de los ojos* means "woman of eyes."

94 A *cante jondo* is a deep song.